Antonio Miguel (Valencia, Spain, 1953), Telecommunications Specialist, Computer Programmer, researcher and scientific disseminator, is a passionate thinker of the philosophy of life and the mysteries of our nature.

In this edition he offers us a collection of reflections that make up a personal philosophy that is as removed from political ideologies as religious ones, all in the spirit of self-improvement and scientific advancement whilst keeping an individual touch and social reality.

A book that bestows upon us a new consciousness through means of a combination of simple and profound reflections in pursuit of the meaning and reason behind our existence.

A frank and penetrating read that provides answers, stimuli and perhaps the discovery of a relevant personal message.

In reality, ourselves, we are God

Antonio Miguel

In reality, ourselves, we are God
Original title: Dios somos nosotros mismos
ISBN: 978-1-329-59689-4

© Original and expanded versions,
2010, 2012, 2014, Antonio Miguel Muñoz.
All rights reserved.

Translation and proofreading
Antonio Miguel,
Juan Carlos Hidalgo.

Photographs
Cover design with artistic impression
of the surface of planet Pluto, original of ESO
(European Southern Observatory), L. Calçada.
Inside photographs:
Maury river, Toroonga river (pages 9 a 13),
Smith Michael L, U.S. Fish and Wildlife,
public-domain-image.com.
Other pages: ESO (European Southern Observatory),
ESA (European Space Agency),
NASA (National Aeronautics and Space Administration),
APLF (Association des planétariums de langue française).

Production
Disfae Ediciones,2015
ediciones@antoniomiguel.es
www.antoniomiguel.es
Sevilla - Spain

International distribution of this edition,
www.amazon.com

In reality, ourselves,
we are God

Index of reflections and references, pages

15 - God / *Reality, life, soul, mind.*

17 - Universe

19 - Man / Energy, *brain, Infinite Intelligence, God.*

21 - Life / *Universe, God.*

23 - Mind / *Brain, human life.*

25 - The Truth

27 - Individuality

29 - Chance and destiny / *Accidents, choices, actions.*

31 - Destiny / *Landmarks, path.*

33 - Chance / *Magic, wisdom, heart.*

35 - Emotions / *Messages.*

37 - Numbers / *Actions, lucky, mathematics, illusion, love.*

39 - Passion / *Message.*

41 - Heart / *Destiny.*

43 - Spirit / *Energy, body, matter, mind.*

45 - Soul

47 - Death / *Existence, eternity, magic, appearance.*

49 - Identity

51 - Capacity / *Defects, qualities, time, possibilities.*

53 - Attitude / *Errors, liberty.*

Reflections and referentes, pages
___

55 - Rebirth

57 - Past, present and future.

59 - Today / *Life, destiny, Universe, dreams.*

61 - Happiness / *Heart.*

63 - Freedom / *Happiness, heart, thought.*

65 - Progress / *Intelligence, love.*

67 - World

69 - Politics and Religion / *Kindness, ideology, progress.*

71 - Generosity

73 - Value the people

75 - Twin Souls / *Inspiration, creativity.*

77 - True love

79 - Blind man's guides

81 - Stones / *Path.*

83 - Life proposals / *Destination, evolution.*

85 - Path / *Nature, opportunities.*

87 - Evolution / *Maturity, wisdom, feelings.*

89 - Enthusiasm / *Life, time, consciousness.*

91 - Confidence

93 - Willpower / *Mind, faith, hope, soul, power.*

95 - Opportunity / *Life, time.*

Reflections and referentes, pages
_____

97 - Wishes / *Chance, dreams, spirit, destiny.*

99 - Illusions

101 - Hits and misses

103 - Luck

105 - The power of emotions / *Dreams, fear, courage, faith.*

107 - Feelings / *Dreams.*

109 - Subconscious / *Happiness.*

111 - Dream / *Life, reality, magic, work, hope.*

113 - Faith / *Mind, Soul, Spirit.*

115 - Idea and reality / *Mind, faith, persistence.*

117 - Imagination / *Reality, existence will.*

119 - Writing / *Freedom, mind, secrets, magic.*

121 - Art / *Soul, message, love.*

123 - The artist

124 - Fantasy / *Reality, creativity, conscience, freedom.*

127 - Reality / *Discover, create, conscience.*

129 - Consciousness / *Energy, existence, destiny.*

131 - Love / *Energy, conscience, will.*

133 - It's all about you / *Happiness, existence, individuality.*

133 - Index of references

Nowadays there is a lot of talk about the non-existence of God as a means of explaining the origin of the Universe, that the soul is an illusion ...

The mind is our universal guide; our purpose: we ourselves and our consequences; the expansion of God into specific and infinite possibilities which stare at each other and at themselves so as to learn to display and transmit their message within a permanent continuity that has neither beginning or end.

Certainly, there is no soul or a mind within a non-existent body. Similar to how the reflection of sunlight in the emptiness of the dry creek does not come in the form of bright sparks, nor be feel the power of the torrent, nor be reflect stars on the surface of the absent waters.

But even without its reflection, light exists; even without the form, the energy flows; and even without the gaze of this existence, the Universe persists: God. Ourselves.

Globular cluster NGC 6397.
ESO

God

God is not a real thing, but all of reality is God: ourselves; of its infinite aspects, a temporal, fleeting expression in this life experience.

Abounding in the possibilities, He is an obligatory accomplice, his spirit is in our soul and his power in our mind.

Artist's impression of the surface of the dwarf planet Makemake.
ESO, L. Calçada, Nick Risinger, skysurvey.org.

Universe

The Universe is an aspect of
God of which we are also part;
and that we can appreciate,
as in extraordinary mirror,
according to our senses, from
the other side of the crystal.

A Snapshot of the Jewel Box cluster with the ESO VLT.
ESO, Y. Beletsky.

Man

Every body is part of the universal energy.

Every mind is a reflection, a small flash of infinite intelligence.

Every soul is a little bit of the spirit of God, and every life is another experiment of old and new laws with new and old messages.

Artist's impression of the planet Beta Pictoris B.
ESO, L. Calçada.

Life

Life is a dialogue with the Universe.
That is to say, with God. And every one
of us is a scattered fragment of Him.

In this way, every existence is a
conversation between the whole and
the part; inexorably at its service, and
an unaware explorer of the infinite thicket
of Being supreme.

Artist's impression of snow lines around TW Hydrae.
ESO, B. Saxton y A. Angelich, NRAO, AUI, NSF, ALMA.

Mind

Body, brain ..., mind?
The mind is something prior
that tries to put on a dress
that appears to be too small.
Why so much effort?
Is like a diver, confined, limited ...

Perhaps to be able to explore
the depth of a new sea: human life.

The mind reminds us
that our true existence
is at the surface.

Celestial scribbled. Area near the Chamaeleon I complex of bright nebulae.

ESO

The truth

Life is somewhat deceiving.
A clever entertainment in
the dismantling of appearance
so that we ourselves find the truth.

Tau Bootis-B exoplanet star.
ESO, Digitized Sky Survey 2.

Individuality

We all have something that is distinct, new, ours, and good.

Each one of us is a unique jewel, unrepeatable, the value of which you will come to understand after taking the time to discover it.

Galaxy Starburst J0-82354-96.
ESA, Hubble & NASA, M. Hayes.

Chance and Destiny

Life is one tremendous continuity
in which everything happens
in the same way, through accidents
that invite us to make decisions.

The events are not what matter,
but rather the subsequent actions.

Make a choice is to live, and every
choice is a new fortune for us.

Image from the APEX telescope. Part of the star formation Taurus Molecular Cloud.
ESO, APEX, MPIFR, OSO, A. Hacar, Digitized Sky Survey 2 / Davide De Martin.

Destiny

To live is to make choices as we learn
to read and transmit the signs of the path
that ourselves we discovered.

A new and uncertain path —to our eyes—,
without judges awaiting. Each step judges
us and condemns us.

Constellation Carina.
NASA

Chance

Chance is the disguise worn by the
magic that accompanies every life,
bypassing wisdom as well as ignorance.
It listens only to the heart.

The peculiar galaxy Centaurus A (NGC 5128).
ESO

Emotions

The actions conscious or subconscious
caused by our emotions shows us,
in new perspectives, the interpretation
of the next message.

Artist's impression of the pulsar PSR J0348+0432 and its white dwarf companion.
ESO, L. Calçada.

Numbers

A precise action, a stroke of luck, a rose ...
Everything that surprises or moves
us is none other than the high art of logic,
the consequence of magnificent
mathematical complexities.

The more important equation is the illusion,
the perfect result: love.

This artist's impression shows how ULAS J1120+0641, a very distant quasar powered by a black hole.
ESO, representación gráfica de M. Kornmesser.

Passion

All passion contains a seed with a message
for the person in whom it is awakened.
A personal reading, extraordinary
and determining for those who
decides to live it.

M1-67 is the youngest wind-nebula around a Wolf-Rayet star, called WR124, in our Galaxy.
ESO

Heart

The decisions of the heart
are what make our destination is truly ours.
And that is what matters.

Galaxi Centaurus A.
ESO, WFI (Óptica) MPIFR, ESO, APEX / A. Weiss, al. Subm. NASA, CXC, CFA / R. Kraft et al. Rayos X.

Spirit

The spirit, a subtle form of universal
energy, makes of our physical body
a sophisticated instrument for
communicating with our material world.
A surprising whole in which the mind
is the nexus and interpreter, the point
of encounter and communication:
the magical cathedral, the temple
of creativity.

The Helix Nebula (NGC 7293).
ESO

The soul

And the soul, a bipolar reflection,
the line of harmony and
the dimensional frontier,
shaping an original arrangement;
a particular frequency.

She's the individual vibration;
the unique, unrepeatable,
universal personality.

Nebula of Orión.
ESO, Igor Chekalin.

Death

We envision our existence
as a novel that shall end in death.

But who are we to designate the
ending to something when we ignore
its original beginning? ...
How to know if this is the story
or just another chapter? ...

I suspect that it is all the theatre
of eternity, always with the same
actors changing only the costumes.

There is no death, only life
and magical appearances.

Galaxi NGC-3621.
ESO

Identity

We are the effects of ourselves;
a mix of imperfections and virtues,
doubts, certainties and emotions,
impressing the minds of others
and perceiving of the particular
interpretations of each one ...
Too many translations for
understanding each other!
And escaping this «day to day»
is very difficult.

Distance and solitude are made
necessary for those who wish to
find themselves.

Planet HD-189733B.
NASA, ESA, M. Kornmesser.

Capacity

We are so worried about our defects
and shortcomings that we often
forget our virtues.

What occurs is similar to what happens
to that tool which, in not being part
of our lives, we end up ignoring.

And that is how we act sometimes,
from a negative point of view,
losing time and possibilities.

The Star area Beta Pictoris.
ESO, Digitized Sky Survey 2189733B.

Attitude

We are not perfect, and we also make mistakes throughout our lives.

But the secret is in our attitude:
don't be a slave to your defects
nor from your mistakes, act freely.
Because life is continuously beginning
and everything starts anew at every
moment. Even now.

Artistic impression of planet Super-Earth orbiting the star GJ 1214.
ESO, L.Calçada.

Rebirth

There are many occasions on which
you can astonish people, but surprising
yourself is a challenge that comes every day.

It is like being reborn; it means growth
through the conquest of your own reality.

Artistic impression of a planet orbiting the star Alpha Centauri B.
ESO, L. Calçada, Nick Risinger (skysurvey.org), Pictoris.

Past, present and future

Every moment is a seed for subsequent moments, and each group of moments yields a different fruit.

We cannot change past events, but we can always choose the combination that we find agreeable: to look at the past in a different way.

You will awaken another present and you will build another future.

Planet Kepler-62, impression artistic.
NASA

Today

Today is the greatest day of your life.

Today is neither «yesterday or tomorrow»; today is the moment for living and working as you wish, for activating the forces that create your destiny.

This is the moment in which your existence is tangible within the Universe, your wishes are heard and your actions bring about compromises within the symphony of the universe.

The dreams and memories are created in the Present.

Sunset over Paranal Observatory, Chile.
ESO, S. Bruni.

Happiness

Happiness is always found accepting,
first, where you are, and then beginning
to walk in the direction dictated by the heart.

There is no other way.

Zodiacal light over the desert of Atacama, Chile.
ESO, Y. Beletsky.

Freedom

Happiness comes from the heart,
and freedom begins in the thought.

The Milky Way glitters brightly over ALMA, in desert of Atacama, Chile.
ESO, B. Tafreshi.

Progress

The Intelligence needs a constant parallel,
a capable catalyst to neutralise the troubling
consequences of its solitary advance: love.

True progress is possible only in this manner.

Artist's impression of how the surface of Pluto.
ESO, L. Calçada.

World

The only way to change your world
is to change yourself.

And change this world of ours,
also begins at this point.

The full Moon and the U.S. Capitol, in the evening on Tuesday, Feb. 7, 2012.
NASA, Bill Ingalls.

Politics and religion

We need not ideologies or religions, only good people.

In a collaborative system and fair interchange, the only religion necessary is kindness, and the only useful ideology: the human progress.

Galaxy spiral NGC-7424.
ESO

Generosity

Give the best of yourself which
you know already and you will find
the best of yourself that you have
yet to discover.

Galaxy Messier 100 and Supernova SN-2006-XN.
ESO, AIF, Danish 1,5 m, R. Gendler, J. E. Ovaldsen, CC. Thöne y C. Féron.

Value the people

Recognising the qualitative aspects of people, to be aware of his reality and transmit to them your positive essence, is the most valuable thing that we can do for them.

The Lupus 3 dark cloud and associated hot young stars.
ESO, F. Comeron.

Twin Souls

From time to time we are faced with
«souls mirror» reflecting, reminding us,
the best of ourselves.

And in trying to embrace them,
the glass breaks into thousand pieces,
thousand sensations; new feelings
of anxiety that are revived, emotions
that bring us back to life, inspirations,
seeds of creativity ...

Afterwards, the time helps us discover
the mystery of this explosion; something
new and special is born, something that
would be impossible without that stumble.

A Cosmic Embrace in the constellation of Canis Major.
ESO

True love

Love is an unconditional surrender in the face of another unconditional surrender. And both add up a beautiful victory.

Cosmic Ballet or Devil's Mask, Galaxy NGC 6769 and 70.
ESO

Blindman's guide

It could happen in instants or in a
matter of years: someone appears
and disappears from your live; and
we ask ourselves about this person ...

And the topic is that the work
has already been done; only had to
guide us to the place where we now
find ourselves.

Asteroid (234) Bárbara, artist's impression.
ESO, L. Calçada.

Stones in our path

There are those who die as were born;
is as if they had been born deads.

And we come across them as like
stones, like immovable rocks, as they
disrupt our path.

Perhaps this is their mission, because
force us to elude them in our travel
and thus, also, do of guides in our path.

Jets coming out from a 24 Jupiter-mass brown dwarf.
ESO

Life's proposals

Sometimes life makes things difficult
for us; it makes suggestions, possibly.

We are not victims of gods or destinies;
through these challenges we pay for
our own particular evolution.

Indeed, in a certain manner, we are
obligated by nature in this way
to discover and operate abilities that,
being dormant in our subconscious,
are often ignored.

The Trifid Nebula.
ESO

Path

Who knows what he wants, sees the
options available. He who does not
know where he is going, don't understand
what he sees.

Like the way in which the wind that
moves and transports leaves and seeds,
nature displaces us in the direction
of potential factors and circumstances.

It is necessary to be alert and acknowledge
them with integrity and honesty, since
they comprise options, opportunities,
rescue bridges ...

Sunset Páranla, Chile, with the Moon and Venus.
ESO, Y. Beletsky.

Evolution

The maturity is the art of utilising
character together with intelligence
and wisely living our emotions.

But the qualitative and vital leap
is to choose your feelings and submit
yourself to them definitively.

Burning lithium inside a star, artist's impression.
ESO, L. Calçada.

Enthusiasm

To lose enthusiasm is to lose life.
It is like lifting one's foot off the accelerator
when we are driving and leaving the car
wandering in «neutral».

To live without enthusiasm is to live by inertia,
and live only by inertia is to lose the time,
emotions and conscience.

A Trio of Super-Earths, artist's impression.
ESO

Confidence

When we think that we know very little, we
lose confidence in the little that we do know.

But the decision is always positive
to find our mistake or affirm our faith.

Artist's impression of the surroundings of the supermassive black hole in NGC 3783.
ESO

Willpower

Willpower is a mental state full of hope that is not far from faith.

A message from the soul with the strength of the spirit: your true power.

Artist's impression of how the surface of Pluto.
ESO, L. Calçada.

Opportunity

It is possible for us to go through our
lives waiting for the right moment,
the right time, the opportunity ...
Without noticing that most things
are obtained in a simple manner:
by beginning to work in the right now.

Globular cluster Messier 4.
ESO, Digitized Sky Survey 2 / Agradecimientos Davide De Martin.

Desires

Sometimes we fail to obtain what we
desire, despite how much we want it.
On the other hand, in making an attempt
and through strange accidents, we find
what we truly need.

Perhaps our dreams, desires and ambitions
can sometimes be like traps; a strategy
of the mind and spirit, the destiny's juggling
act, to put what we truly need in front
of our eyes: to one step.

Cluster open Trumpler-16.
NASA, ESA y Jesús Maíz Apellániz / Instituto de Astrofísica de Andalucía, España.

Illusions

The mistaken illusions have the same sense
as the illusions successful.

They are to entertain and instruct us
while the real illusions arrive.

Star formation in the Large Magellanic Cloud.
ESA, NASA.

Successes and failures

Life is the partial framework
of a canvas without edges or seams,
a tapestry without a bad stitch.

There are no successes and failures,
every personal mistake is also another
opportune and necessary stitch.

Eclipse, virtual representation.
NASA

Luck

Luck exists because you believe in it,
for nothing exists in your mind
that you do not believe exists,
and every moment of your life
is an attempt to harmonise the reality
with the thoughts.

Artist's impression of a gas giant planet forming in the disc around the young star HD 100546.
ESO, L. Calçada.

The power of emotions

Some people live according to their aspirations and others live according to their fears.

The fear will create the alternatives to your dreams; the value and faith, the opportunities.

Milky Way.
NASA, JPL-Caltech / ESO, R. Daño.

Feelings

Reality gives life or kills one's dreams,
paving the way for new ones in
a continuous rotation in which our
feelings survive; they are what counts.

This artist's impression shows the supergiant star Betelgeuse.
ESO, L. Calçada.

Subconscious

Every man has dominion over his own self if he develops the ability to voluntarily influence his subconscious. This is a mechanism of perfect solutions based on the elements that have been able to reach them.

A magnificent tool for building one's misfortunes as well as happiness.

The glowing cloud Sharpless 2-296, part of the Seagull Nebula.
ESO

Dreams

Dreaming is a necessity.
Even more, an obligation.

Dreaming is inseparable from life; it is the chemistry of reality, the meaning of existence and the first step towards a higher state of being.

Dreaming is not the recourse of consolation, it is the seed of work and hope. To dream is to put the spirit into motion and to begin to create, to generate extraordinary energy out of our personal magic.

To abandon our dreams is to submit our lives to those who do not renounce dreaming.

Gamma-ray burst, artist's impression.
ESO, L. Calçada.

Faith

In the jungle of the mind, faith is
the path of certainty, the path protected
from attacks waged by concern, by
hypothetical limitations, and the
conditionings, where the strength of
the soul is action.

Desire, impulse, feeling, mental status ...
A final attitude as absent of emotions,
because they are all balanced in perfect
harmony with the spirit and the environment;
an attitude they can turn into occurrences,
into direct and concrete actions.

The Hibernating Stellar Magnet, artist's impression.
ESO, L. Calçada.

Idea and reality

An idea is made reality when it takes
on a concrete form within the mind,
and merge all faculties according
to the impulse of your desire, until
the level of faith and persistence
reached no longer allow for failure
as a final point.

How jets from supermassive black holes could form galaxies, artist's impression.
ESO, L. Calçada.

Imagination

Everything is dependent upon its origin.
Therefore, there can be nothing within that
which does not follow the same logic.

Thought is one aspect of reality,
and all conjecture can be crystallised;
it existed, exists and will exist.

The farthest known planetoid sun, artist's impression.
NASA, ESA y Adolf Schallerl.

Writing

There is no equal alternative;
writing is the kingdom of liberty,
because it is the most faithful
a reflection of mind.

All shapes, colours, melodies...
and mysteries, without limits,
are in the mind.

Writing is a magical instrument
for discovering secrets,
not only for the reader
but also for the writer who,
in a strange way,
turns into the scrivener.

Glass of ice water, in orbit, outside of a planetary system, impression.
APLF, ESO.

Art

Sometimes we feel that something
is taking us to mysterious and happy
states of mind ... remembering instinctively
the soul of lost gods that beats inside each
and every one of us; an soul desperate to
return his house; to the magical home
that we abandoned long ago in a strange
outburst.

Art is that which revives us, albeit for a
fraction of a second, the divinity that we
do not wish to lose definitively; a love letter
telling us that not all is lost, that the heavens
continue to await the best from us.

Snapshot of the Jewel Box cluster, Field of Jewel.
ESO

The artist

The artist is a daring «Don Juan»
of the difficult task of coexisting
with his or her lovers:

the reason and the passion,
the physical and the ethereal ...
each instant that dies and
the always living eternity.

Fantasy

Fantasy does not take us away from reality,
but that it gets us closer to it,
to its truth and to its secrets.
Imagination is necessary in order to invent;
and what is invent but discover?...
And if create is to design that which not exists,
to build new realities, is it possible
to do this without dreaming?...

I hear my bird sing in the balcony,
and I wonder if will be aware of the beauty
of its song, or its existence.
I whistle and it responds every day when I feed it.
Can he imagine a life outside its cage?
Would he want it?

I get close and ask it:
«Have you got feelings, do you dream?»...
I open its cage and he it attempts
to close it with its beak.
Surprised, I remove my gaze from that prison
that is its house and head out to the street,
and watch traffic, the urban racket ...
and think that perhaps we also do the same.
How many books we close,
how many feelings we separate,
and how many dreams we forget!

Spacecraft Soyuz
NASA

Deep down, we have what we are seeking;
we insist on eating, we sing to forget,
and we stay inside the cage of our fears,
dead in life, like incorrupt cadavers.

The time makes us myopic faced with our lies,
our barriers, until one day,
when already too late,
we impact with them.

I distance myself from my coward bird,
and also wish to distance myself
from the reality of every day,
I prefer the truth of my fantasy.

The role is waiting for me on the table,
like a white horse ready to be mounted
and rid by your side:
«Yes, I return to you, dear fantasy,
eternal lover and faithful companion ...
I do not know where you will take me,
but without you I have already understood
to where you are going: the closing of life's door,
to live without awareness, to love not truly,
to chirp in order to eat and in order to forget;
to forget freedom.».

Simulation of how a gas cloud that has been observed approaching the supermassive black hole at the centre of the galaxy.
ESO, MPE, Marc Schartmann.

Reality

The instrument produces,
the musician execute, the composer creates ...
But the notes antedate everything else,
and all compositions are a reality
that suddenly we discover.

Naive of me; thought that I was creating
and believed who was thinking,
but I merely read what
I think and draw what I see.
What book opens to my reading,
and what scenery appears in my sight? ...

I explore the eternal immensity,
navigating the sea of possibilities
without knowing if I am the captain or sailor,
which light guides me and which port.

Discover, create ... What is reality? ...
Just a moment ago, in recent days,
in recent years, from the time I was born,
and even since before that time,
myriad circumstances have occurred
for that I might ask myself about the truth.

I too was a possibility and now
I am consciousness.
This is the only response.

Image of the famous early-type spiral galaxy Messier 104, widely known as the Sombrero.
ESO, AIF, Danish, 1,5 m, R. Gendler y J. E. Ovaldsen.

Consciousness

We are energy that has been imprisoned
and transformed through organic chemistry;
we are individual, unique experiments ...
And then we try to understand us.

Energy is not created or destroyed,
and we avail ourselves of its conversion.
What is the purpose of our existence?
Who benefits our conversion? ...
If we are energy then we will always exist,
and human beings are just merely
«one state of affairs». Will we preserve
after our nuances, our consciousness? ...

Perhaps there is no «an before», and we are merely
a temporary flow of ongoing continuities and
an infinite number of variables within which
consciousness is a new property,
harvest of the human manifestation.

We developed organs that we need
and inhibit those that we do not utilise ...
Is consciousness the most sophisticated
and delicate organ of our existential anguish?

Perhaps we will not find «an after»,
be it as an objective, result or benefit ...
and to create an ending, a universal destiny,
likely is a pending issue
for which we are responsible.

Gamma-ray burst, artist's impression.
ESO

Love

If energy comes first,
and then matter, chemistry ...,
is it consciousness or love
that comes after? ...

But love without consciousness
is not true love;
because is the conscious
will what brings dignity to delivery
and value of the action.

Is love, therefore, energy
at an superior stage? ...
Or is it the ending and the beginning,
the return to a the previous state:
primeval and creator?

Everything is within you

_____

Dear friend, did you feel happy with this morning's
coffee?... And when you were looking at your garden's
green grass?, when you look at your loved ones?...
On the way to work, to school, or to your other
obligations? ...

Happiness is not in any one of those things,
for they only provide reflections of what you have
within you.

You know?, you could not be here, listening to me,
contemplating. But it happens that you're;
in this world, to living out this life
without knowing why, or for what.

Do not hesitate, the Heavens expect something
from you, of your strange existence.
«What?», you might ask yourself ...
«I, a tiny thing within the immensity of the Universe,
what can I do?, what have I got for to offer?».

The Universe expects from you everything
that you can give. In the child, a smile; in your brother,
a hug; in your neighbour, the friendly greeting; in your
partner, love, faithfulness; in your work,
eagerness; in your dreams, will ...
And perhaps some more things.

Remember that nothing is the same.
Words can be the same, but the essence is of each.
We are unique; each of us is unrepeatable.

Nobody will ever have your eyes,
nobody will ever have your warmth,
nobody will ever love as you.
And your smile will never again exist.
If we have come to see your smile
it is thanks to you.

Forget the sadness of that love that never was,
of the dreams that did not come to pass,
of those things that you should have done.

None of that not happen for the purpose
of bringing about the occurrence
of what ended up happening,
for the purpose of living out
other dreams and do other things.

Because, in reality, that is what you are,
what each one of us is:
what we can still become,
what we are still able to love,
what we are still able to do.

Thematic index

Themes	Pages
Appearance	47
Art	121
Artist	123
Attitude	53
Brain	19, 23
Capacity	51
Chance	97
Collaboration	69
Confidence	91
Consciousness	89, 124, 127, 129, 131
Creativity	75, 124, 127
Death	47
Destination	29, 31, 41, 59, 83, 97, 129
Dreams	59, 97, 105, 107, 111
Elections	29
Emotions	35, 105
Energy	19, 43, 129, 131
Enthusiasm	89
Errors	53, 101
Eternity	47
Evolution	83, 87
Existence	47, 117, 129, 133
Faith	93, 105, 113, 115
Fantasy	124
Fear	105
Feelings	87, 107
Freedom	53, 63, 119, 124
Future	55
Generosity	71
God	13, 15, 19, 21
Goodness	69
Happiness	61, 63, 107, 133
Heart	33, 41, 61, 63
Hope	93, 111
Ideology	69
Illusions	37, 99
Imagination	115, 117
Individuality	27, 133
Inspiration	75
Intelligence	19, 65, 87

Life	15, 21, 23, 59, 83, 89, 111
Love	37, 65, 77, 121, 131
Luck	37, 103
Magic	33, 47, 111, 119
Mathematics	37
Matter	43
Maturity	87
Message	35, 39, 121
Mind	13, 15, 23, 43, 93, 103, 113, 115, 119
Nature	83, 85
Numbers	37
Opportunity	85, 95, 105
Passion	39
Past	55
Path	31, 81, 85
Persistence	115
Policy	69
Possibilities	51
Power	93, 105
Present	55
Progress	65, 69
Qualities	51, 83
Random	29, 33
Rating	73, 105
Reality	15, 111, 115, 117, 124, 127
Religion	69
Soul	13, 15, 45, 75, 93, 113, 121
Soul mates	75
Spirit	13, 15, 43, 93, 97, 113
Subconscious	107
Thought	63, 103
Time	51, 89
Today	59
Truth	25
Universe	13, 15, 17, 21, 59
Willpower	93, 117, 131
Wisdom	33, 87
Wishes	97
Work	111
World	67
Writing	119

www.ingramcontent.com/pod-product-compliance
Lightning Source LLC
Chambersburg PA
CBHW040455240426
43663CB00033B/17